TWENTY PROGRESSIVE SOLOS FOR STRING INSTRUMENTS
(For individual and multiple solo players)

Transcribed for String Instruments and Piano
by SAMUEL APPLEBAUM

Foreword

These solos, with piano accompaniment, can be used by individual players as well as for performance by multiple players. They may also be played in unison by violins, violas and cellos. As multiple solos they have proven effective for recruiting string players in the public schools, and for string classes, solo contests and string festivals.

Each piece has a distinct value, either for development of certain rhythms, for the development of the left hand and bow arm, and for development of style and musicianship. For more advanced players, these pieces may include shifting into the third position. The third position fingerings may be added by the student or the teacher.

Contents

E.L. 2733

To a Wild Rose

(Edward MacDowell)

Bass

Transcribed for Bass and Piano by
Samuel Applebaum

*) The measures are numbered according to phrases. This will be helpful in memorizing.

Leave a slight pause for phrasing at each comma (,) with the bow remaining on the string.

**) Lift the bow at each (//) and start down bow on the next note.

EL 2733

Whispering Hope

(Alice Hawthorne)

Transcribed for Bass and Piano by
Samuel Applebaum

*) The dash indicates a smooth détaché bowing. Move the bow a bit faster for each note.
**) The measures are numbered according to phrases. This will be helpful in memorizing.

EL 2733

Chop Sticks

Transcribed for Bass and Piano by
Samuel Applebaum

(a) Use the martelé stroke (above the middle) the first time and col legno the second time. For the col legno, strike the strings with the bow stick slightly above the middle of the bow.

(b) The lower notes may be left out.

(c) ⌢ = a slight pause to allow enough time for the proper bow grip.

(d) The notes marked with crosses (+) are played pizzicato with the left hand.

EL 2733

Rigaudon *)

(Peter Lee of Putney)
First published 1785

Transcribed for Bass and Piano by
Samuel Applebaum

*) A Rigaudon (or rigadoon) is a 17th century dance usually in 4/4 time. It was used in the operatic ballets of Rameau and also adopted in the suites of Purcell, Bach, etc. as well as by modern composers.

**) The dashes mean a smooth détaché. (⸗) means détaché lancé - smooth notes with a slight pause between each.

EL 2733

The Little French Boy

Jean B. Senaille
(1687-1730)

Transcribed for Bass and Piano by
Samuel Applebaum

Allegro con brio

ⓐ Use a martele stroké for the notes marked with dots, and a broad smooth detache for thosé marked with dashes.

EL 2733

Along the Brook

(H. Lichner)

Transcribed for Bass and Piano by
Samuel Applebaum

ⓐ Leave a slight pause at each comma with the bow remaining on the string.

ⓑ Lift the bow smoothly at each (∥) and start down bow on the next note.

Wedding of the Winds

(Concert Waltz)
John T. Hall

Transcribed for Bass and Piano by
Samuel Applebaum

(a) Lift the bow at each (//) and start down bow at the next note.

While Strolling Through the Park One Day

Transcribed for Bass and Piano by
Samuel Applebaum

ⓐ The notes marked with dashes are to be played broadly, using a smooth detaché stroke. For the notes marked with dots, use the martelé stroke, keeping the bow on the string.

ⓑ Lift the bow and start down bow at each (⫽).

ⓒ Leave a slight pause for phrasing at each (ⸯ).

EL 2733

A Day with the Gypsies

(Fr. Behr)

Transcribed for Bass and Piano by
Samuel Applebaum

ⓐ Lift the bow at each (∥) and start down bow on the next note.

EL 2733

The Caissons Go Rolling Along

Brig. Gen. Edmund L. Gruber

Transcribed for Bass and Piano by
Samuel Applebaum

(a) The notes marked with crosses (+) are to be played pizzicato with the left hand.

(b) Lift the bow at each (//), and start down bow on the next note.

(c) The measures are numbered according to phrases. This will be helpful in memorizing.

EL 2733

March Militaire

(Franz Schubert)

Transcribed for Bass and Piano by
Samuel Applebaum

D.C. al Fine

(To Konrad Efrem Tree)

The Four Pipers

Passepied in Rondo Form*
Andre Destouches (1672-1749)

Transcribed for Bass and Piano by
Samuel Applebaum

*) A Passepied is a lively old French dance somewhat like a minuet. A Rondo is a form consisting of a repeated refrain with different "couplets" - ABACADAE.

EL 2733

D (Couplet III)

E (Couplet IV)

A Presto

Tulip

(Heinrich Lichner Op. 111, No. 4)

Transcribed for Bass and Piano by
Samuel Applebaum

ⓐ Use the martelé stroke for the notes marked with dots. The notes marked with dashes are to be played broadly.

ⓑ Leave a slight pause for phrasing at each (ⁱ).

ⓒ Lift the bow and start down bow at each (⫽).

EL 2733

The Little Princess

James Hook
(First published in 1785)

Transcribed for Bass and Piano by
Samuel Applebaum

Lily

(C. H. Lichner)

Transcribed for Bass and Piano by
Samuel Applebaum

Gertrude's Dream Waltz

(L. Van Beethoven)

Transcribed for Bass and Piano by
Samuel Applebaum

Gypsy Dance

(H. Lichner)

Transcribed for Bass and Piano by
Samuel Applebaum

*) The measures are numbered according to phrases. This will be helpful in memorizing.
**) The notes marked with crosses (+) are to be played pizzicato with the left hand.

EL 2733

24

Spanish Dance

(M. Moszkowski, Op. 12, No. 1)

Transcribed for Bass and Piano by
Samuel Applebaum

ⓐ Lift the bow at each (⫽).
ⓑ The notes marked with crosses (+) are to be played pizzicato with the left hand. The open D is to be plucked with the 4th finger.
ⓒ B.M. = below the middle of the bow: W.B. = whole bow: A.M. = above the middle.

EL 2733

Minute Waltz

(Fr. Chopin, Op. 64, No. 1)

Transcribed for Bass and Piano by
Samuel Applebaum

*) Play as rapidly as possible without sacrificing clarity or evenness. Listen carefully to the intonation partifularly to the half steps. Practice slowly at first, gradually increasing the speed.

EL 2733

Ninette at Court

Louis Saint-Amans (1749-1820)

Transcribed for Bass and Piano by
Samuel Applebaum

*) These eighth notes are to be played smoothly below the middle of the bow, with the wrist and
finger stroke. Use about 2 inches of bow.

EL 2733

Meno mosso